SCHIRMER'S LIBRARY
OF MUSICAL CLASSICS

LUDWIG van BEETHOVEN

Sonata

For Violin and Piano

T0053071

The Violin Part
Edited and Fingered by

ADOLPH BRODSKY

The Piano Part Edited by

MAX VOGRICH

Complete (10 Sonatas) — Library Vol. 232

Separately

Sonata, Op. 24   — Library Vol. 468

Sonata, Op. 47 (*Kreutzer*) — Library Vol. 74

ISBN 0-7935-6417-4

G. SCHIRMER, Inc.

DISTRIBUTED BY

HAL•LEONARD®
CORPORATION
7777 W. BLUEMOUND RD. P.O. BOX 13819 MILWAUKEE, WI 53213

SONATA.
Op. 24.

Sonata 5.

L. van Beethoven.

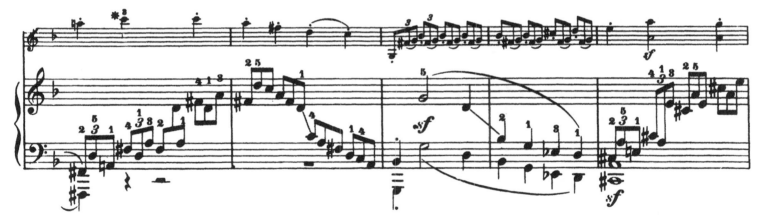

*C appears in origi-
nal ms. but D was
possibly intended.

29523

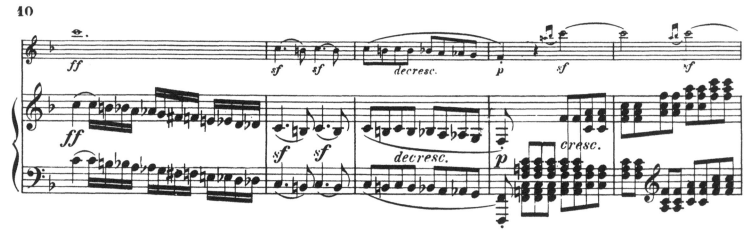

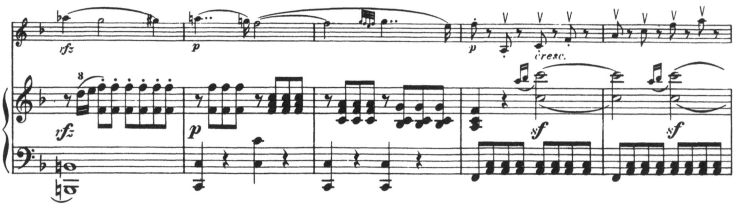

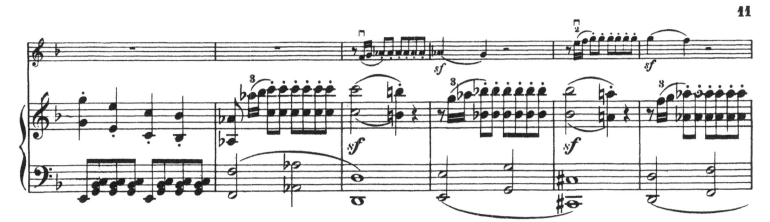

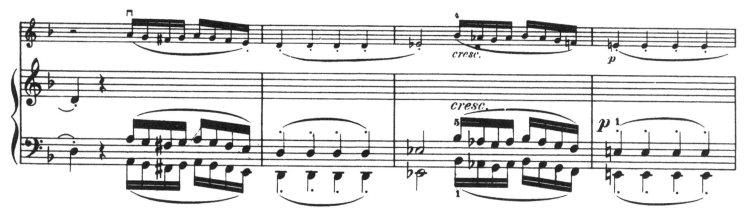

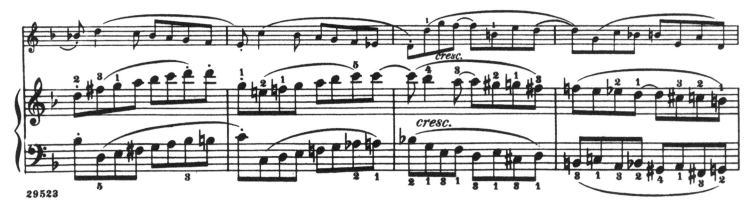

29523

Adagio molto espressivo.

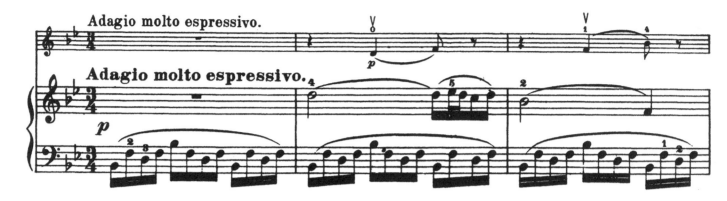

Adagio molto espressivo.

SONATA.
Op. 24.

VIOLIN.

L. van Beethoven.

Allegro.

Sonata 5.

VIOLIN.

*C appears in original ms. but D was possibly intended.

VIOLIN.

Adagio molto espressivo.

VIOLIN.

Rondo.
Allegro ma non troppo.

VIOLIN.

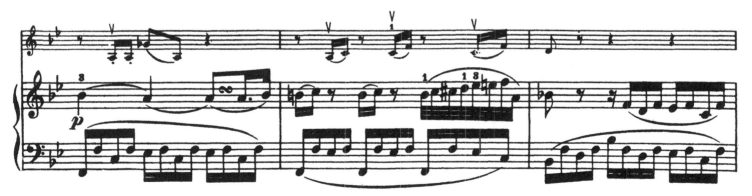

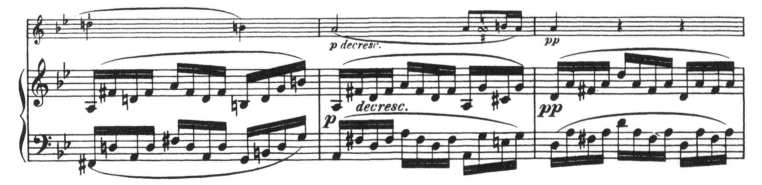

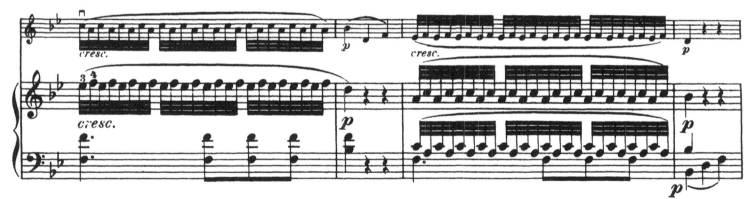

29523

Scherzo.
Allegro molto.

Allegro molto.
La prima parte senza repetizione.

p

Fine.

Fine.

Trio.

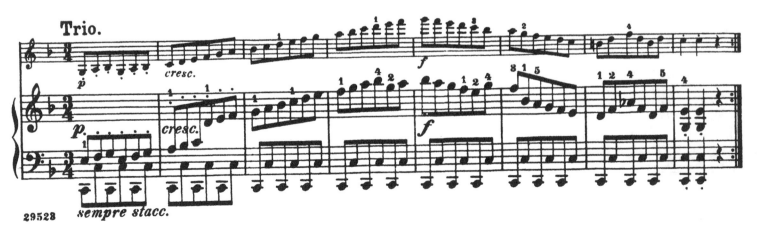

sempre stacc.

Rondo.
Allegro ma non troppo.

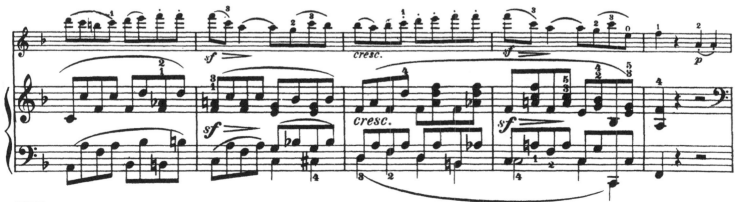

29523

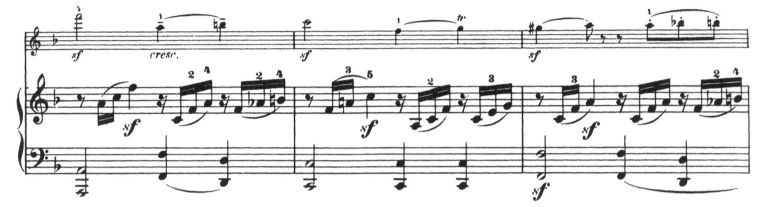